DEC   1998

DATE DUE

VOLLEYBALL
BASICS OF THE GAME

ZACHARY A. KELLY

The Rourke Corporation, Inc.
Vero Beach, Florida 32964

PHOTO CREDITS:
All photos © Tony Gray except © Tony Duffy (NBC/Allsport): pages 7; © Holly McPeak (NBC/Allsport): page 8; © Rick Stewart (NBC/Allsport): page 11; © East Coast Studios: page 4

JUDGE ILLUSTRATIONS:
Jim Spence

PROJECT EDITORS:
Harold Lockheimer
Connie Denaburg

EDITORIAL SERVICES:
Penworthy Learning Systems

Library of Congress Cataloging-in-Publication Data

Kelly, Zachary A., 1970-
    Volleyball—basics of the game / Zachary A. Kelly.
        p. cm. — (Volleyball)
    Includes index.
    Summary: Describes the origin of volleyball, basic techniques of the game, equipment involved, and offensive and defensive strategies.
        ISBN 0-86593-504-1
        1. Volleyball—Juvenile literature. [1. Volleyball.] I. Title II. Series:
Kelly, Zachary A., 1970-   Volleyball.
QV1015.3.K45 1998
796.325—dc21   98–23317
                                                                              CIP
                                                                              AC

Printed in the USA

TABLE OF CONTENTS

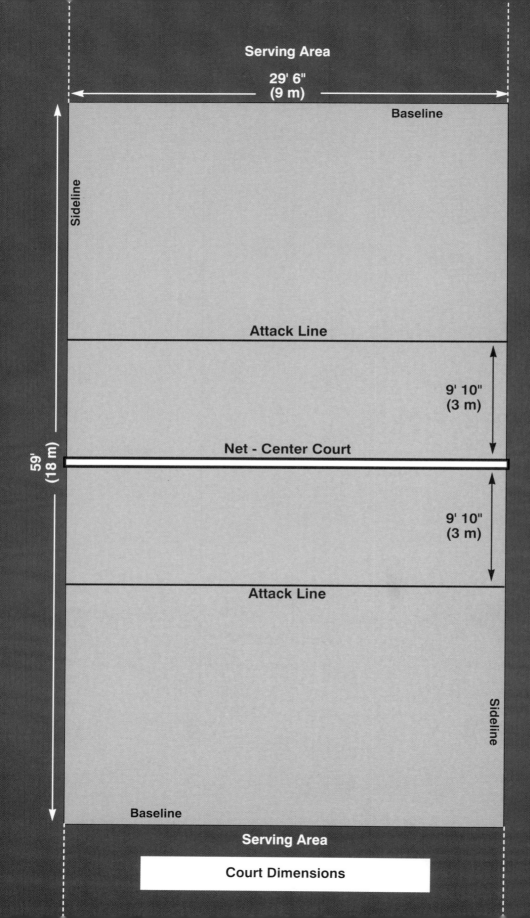

Court Dimensions

THE GAME OF VOLLEYBALL

In the 1984 Olympics, volleyball became an important sport in the United States. It was the first year our teams ever won a medal, and in fact we won two that year. Before then, many Americans did not know much about volleyball. Now people are playing it more than ever.

Volleyball is a team sport. Most volleyball teams have six people, but the number on a side can range from two to six players.

In beach volleyball, for instance, there are now two, three, four, or six person teams. Most indoor volleyball games, however, have six players per team. The two teams face each other on a court divided by a net. The goal is to **volley** the ball across the net so that it hits the floor on the other team's side of the court. The other team wants to keep the ball from hitting their floor and send it back. Winning requires communication and cooperation among teammates.

Over 46 million Americans play volleyball regularly. In many countries, it is the second favorite sport, after soccer. You can find teams at colleges, schools, churches, and community organizations. Over 800 million people play volleyball all over the world.

History of Volleyball

Volleyball was created in 1895 by a man named William G. Morgan who worked for the YMCA in Holyoke, Massachusetts. He wanted a game that would be easy for middle-aged businessmen to play, so he developed a game called *mintonette*. A year later, someone watching the game saw the players hit, or volley, the ball across the net. That person

★ **DID YOU KNOW?**

The first national volleyball championship took place in Brooklyn, NY, in 1922. It was sponsored by the YMCA.

USA Olympics player Yoko Zetterlund prepares to tip the ball.

A beach volleyball player performs an emergency dig.

suggested that a better name for the game was "volleyball." Mr. Morgan agreed, and that has been the name ever since.

When volleyball began it had some very different rules. For example, there could be any number of players on each team. The ball they used was the inside of a basketball. Many rules came from sports like basketball and baseball. For example, the game included dribbling and a team was allowed three outs before losing the ball. Over time, volleyball spread and developed and the YMCA took the game across the United States. Missionaries and soldiers took it to other countries. As more people played, they helped develop it into the game it is today.

★ DID YOU KNOW?

The first World Championships were held in former Czechoslovakia, in Prague.

Volleyball and Other Sports

In many ways, volleyball today is similar to other sports. The court in volleyball is like a tennis court. Both sports have a net in the middle of the court. Both sports **serve** the ball from the back of the court. The court can be made of various materials in both sports, too. The teamwork players use in volleyball is a lot like basketball.

Players call for the ball, have positions to play, and help each other to make shots. While volleyball is similar to some sports, it is also quite different.

In most sports, players try to keep the ball in their team's control as long as possible. Volleyball players have a time limit for ball possession—they are limited by the number of hits they are allowed to make before returning the ball to the other side. Another difference is that volleyball players usually do not touch each other. Most other sports have some contact between players, but volleyball does not.

Junior players gather for a game in their school gymnasium.

An Olympic player performs the advanced jump serve.

Getting Started

One organization governs volleyball: the United States of America Volleyball (USAV). The USAV has an adult program for men and women, as well as a juniors program for boys and girls. It sponsors competitions and helps raise money for the sport. The USAV also helps establish the rules for the country and works with organizations around the world, including Olympic committees. Some groups, such as the U.S. Youth Volleyball League , work only with children. High school students and college students also have their own organizations.

If you are interested in playing volleyball, it is easy to get started. Over 12,000 high schools in the United States have teams. Many junior high schools have teams as well. Most YMCA and local parks and recreational divisions run youth and adult leagues. The easiest way to start is to ask your coach at school about teams in your area—and get going!

THE COURT
AND EQUIPMENT

The Court

   You only need a few pieces of equipment to play volleyball: a court with a high net, a ball, and the right clothes. Finding a court to play on is the first step. There are many different kinds of courts in volleyball. People play on indoor courts and outdoor courts. Most volleyball courts are on wood floors, like in a high school gym. Other surfaces that volleyball can be played on include rubber, sand, and sport court.

Sport court is a surface that can be laid down on top of any other flooring to create a volleyball court. All official courts, though, have one thing in common: they share the same measurements.

Official volleyball courts are 59 feet (18 meters) long and 29 feet 6 inches (9 meters) wide. The **center line** divides the court into two equal playing areas, and the net runs across it. Sidelines and end lines (also known as baselines) show the boundaries of the court. The **attack lines,** or 10 foot lines, mark an area near the net where players make most of their offensive moves. These lines run 9 feet 10 inches (3 meters) away from the center line. The service area includes the entire area behind the court and between the side boundaries.

The Net

Volleyball borrows its net from tennis. When Mr. Morgan created the game, he took a tennis net and raised it to a height just above an average man's head. The original net was 6 feet 6 inches (2 meters). Players had to pass the ball over the net, as in tennis.

★ **COACH'S CORNER**

Crossing the center line is the most common cause of ankle injuries in volleyball. Watch out! Stay safe!

Since the beginning, rules about the net itself have changed and developed into the standards we use today. In women's volleyball, the standard net height is 7 feet 4 inches (2.24 meters) above the floor.

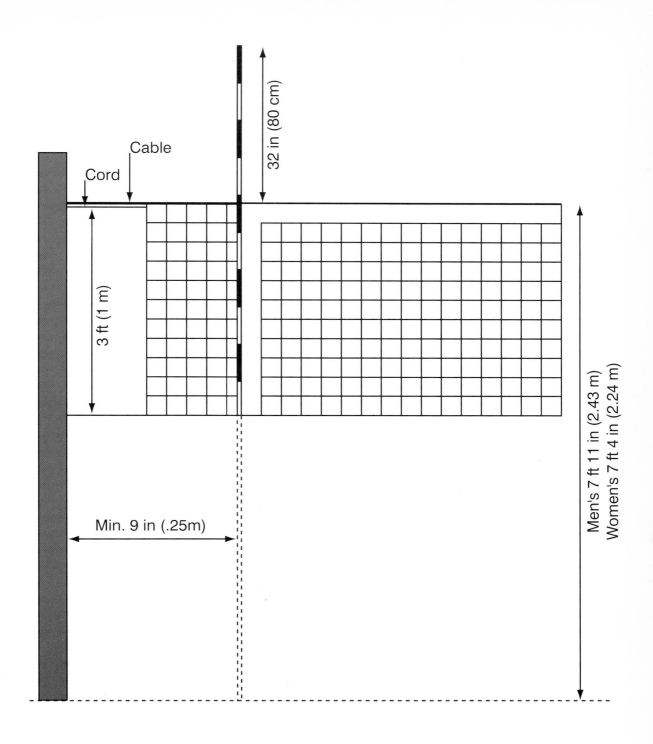

This diagram shows net dimensions.

Play around the net is more aggressive due to the net height.

The net in men's volleyball and coed volleyball (where men and women play together) is 7 feet 11 inches (2.43 meters) high. The height of the net was set to force jumping and high-posture play, which calls for more action around the net. Officials also added two markers, called antennae, to the net above the sidelines. Antennae act as imaginary extensions of the sidelines to help make the boundaries clear in plays above the net.

The Ball

The ball that players use in the game is unique. When volleyball began, players used the air bladder of a basketball. But this ball was too light to be much of a challenge. The players tried a basketball, but they found it was too heavy to hit without catching. In the year 1900, a person named A. G. Spalding watched the game and decided to solve the problem. Mr. Spalding (who founded the sports equipment company of the same name) invented the ball we call the volleyball.

★ COACH'S CORNER

Never catch the ball. Contact it and keep it moving. Don't let it rest on your hands or arms.

The standard volleyball weighs only 9 or 10 ounces (about 270 grams), which makes it easy to hit with the forearm or hands. It is a sphere, about 12 inches (30.5 centimeters) in diameter.

The outside of the ball is covered with strips of leather in a pattern of 12 or 18 strips. Although there are no laces, the texture of the leather and the pattern of the strips make a good texture for controlling the ball. Indoor balls are usually white, while balls for beach games vary in color.

Volleyballs used indoors are white and weigh only 9 or 10 ounces.

In volleyball, personal equipment is kept to a minimum.

Personal Equipment

Volleyball began as a sport that did not require much personal equipment. Even now the average player needs only three basic pieces of personal gear. The first is a pair of good athletic shoes. It takes jumping, stopping short, sprinting and a lot of footwork to play a good game of volleyball. Kneepads are another piece of personal gear that help when the playing gets intense. Most players use kneepads during indoor games to protect their knees if they fall while hitting the ball. And every player needs comfortable clothing. Athletic shorts and t-shirts are the best for practice and informal play, but competition players usually have special uniforms with numbers on them.

Many companies manufacture personal equipment specifically for volleyball players. Always try the gear on to make sure it fits properly and will not restrict your play.

BASIC PLAY AND RULES

Six players usually make up a team on the volleyball court. Three players play the front row, or forward positions, and three play the back row positions. The team rotates one position clockwise each time the service (the team serving the ball) changes. These positions are important to the play, because different positions have different rules and different responsibilities. In beach volleyball, some teams have only two players.

They only rotate their serving order, but they can play any position on the court and usually specialize as a right side or a left side player.

The right **back court** player is the server. This player begins the volley by hitting the ball over the net to the other side. After the serve, players can move anywhere on the court. The server and the other back court players in front of the 10-foot (attack) line normally stay behind the attack line, because they cannot jump and attack a **front court** ball which is above the net if they are in a back court rotation. Front court players often make most of the offensive plays in a volley. A back court player can, if he or she remains behind the 10-foot (attack) line, jump to hit a ball.

Matches and Scoring Points

Competitive volleyball is played in matches. In a collegiate match, the teams are scheduled to play five games against each other. The team that is first to win three of those games wins the match. Tournament, high school, and youth matches are usually shorter, and a team needs to win only two games out of three. To win a game, a team must score 15 points and have a two point lead

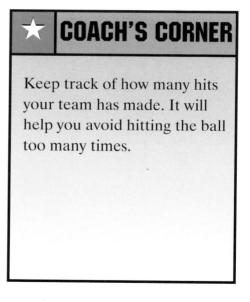

★ **COACH'S CORNER**

Keep track of how many hits your team has made. It will help you avoid hitting the ball too many times.

REPLAY

SUBSTITUTION

TIMEOUT

BALL OUT OF BOUNDS

TOUCH ON BLOCK

END OF GAME OR MATCH

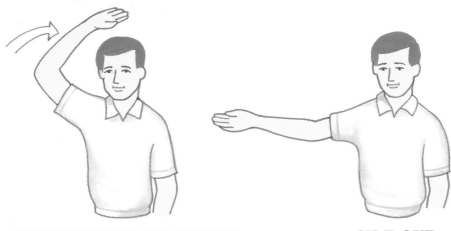

AUTHORIZATION OF SERVICE   **SIDE-OUT**

POINT   **CAUGHT OR THROWN BALL (LIFT)**

BALL CONTACTED MORE THAN THREE TIMES BY A TEAM   **BALL ILLEGALLY CONTACTED MORE THAN ONCE BY A PLAYER**

If a team reaches 15 points but is not two points ahead, the game continues until one team reaches 17 points, and wins the game.

Match rules may specify a 17-point cap to a game. This means the first team to 17 is the winner and does not have to win by 2 points.

In regular play, only the team serving the ball can score. If they win the volley they started, they score a point. If the serving team loses a volley, they must give the ball to the other team. This is a **side-out**, and neither team scores.

Another way of scoring is rally scoring. Officials use this scoring in the last game of a match or in tournament play. In rally scoring, every volley scores a point for the team that wins it.

COACH'S CORNER

When you have to reach to receive the ball, make sure you are not leaning on another player or object to contact it.

Beginning a Volley

To begin a volley, one side serves the ball to the other. This means that the server (the right back court player) tosses the ball up and hits it across the net to the other side. The server must follow specific rules. He or she must begin the serve within five seconds after the referee signals to begin. The server can serve the ball from anywhere behind the baseline. The ball must pass completely over the net during a serve.

The ball cannot touch the net or the antennae at the sides of the net during a serve. The ball cannot contact the ceiling or ceiling obstacles.

The other players must follow certain rules during the serve as well. Each player on both teams must be in his or her position before the serve. You cannot overlap those next to you side to side, or those in front of you front to back, until the ball is served. If someone is out of position, this is called being out of rotation. A referee corrects this error by awarding the other team, if serving, a point. If the opposing team were receiving it would be a side-out.

This player serves to begin a volley.

A hitter sets the ball for an attack.

After the server hits the ball, the players can take any position on the court. The server must hit the ball across the net, unassisted, to the other team.

Hitting and Losing the Ball

Once the ball is in the air, the players can only touch or hit it, not catch it. If the ball rests momentarily on the hands or forearms, the referee will call a **lift** which is a fault and results in a point or side-out. A player can use any part of the body above and including the knee to hit the ball.

Each player and team can hit the ball only a certain number of times in one volley. A player cannot make two hits in a row. This also results in a fault and a loss of the volley. After a hit, another player must make contact with the ball before the first player can hit it again. Each team has three hits to send the ball back across the net. Four hits if a block is involved.

A team can lose a volley four ways. If a player hits the ball twice in a row, or the team hits it more than three times, that team loses the volley. If the player hits the ball out of bounds, the other team wins the volley. If the ball touches the floor, it is dead; and the team that allowed it to hit the floor loses the volley. A **spike** that hits the floor of the other team is called a kill.

OFFENSE AND DEFENSE

The basic offensive move in volleyball is called the
attack or spike. A team is ready to attack its opponent
after it either receives the serve or defends against the
opponent's attack. Strong attacks require strong
teamwork. A team usually comes in contact with the ball
three times as it prepares for an attack: first when it is
received and passed to the **setter**, second when it is set to
the hitter, and third when the **hitter** attacks or spikes
the ball.

Setting and hitting are important jobs on a team. Any team member can be a setter or hitter, and the jobs may rotate from player to player during a game, or each player may be designated as a setter or a hitter. The hitter is a player who has the job of spiking the ball over the net against the opponent. Teams usually designate, or name, players as hitters or setters. The setter's job is to pass, or "set," the ball to the hitter. The setter works hard to set the ball in a way that helps the hitter make a good hit. A setter may have two or three hitters at the net at any given time.

Simple and Complex Offense

There are two types of attack in volleyball. The first is called the two-hitter, or simple, offense. This type of attack puts two hitters and one setter in a row in the front court. The remaining three players defend the back court against balls that break through the front three players. The main advantage of the two-hitter offense is that it is easy to perform. On the other hand, only two hitters are at the net, which limits the options for attack.

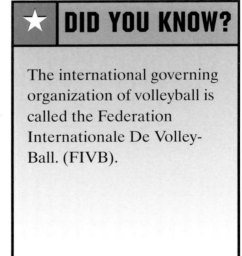

★ **DID YOU KNOW?**

The international governing organization of volleyball is called the Federation Internationale De Volley-Ball. (FIVB).

Back court players scramble to set the ball.

Front court player jumps to spike a perfect set.

The second attack position is called the three-hitter, or complex, offense. The three-hitter attack places three hitters in the front court. The setter stays in the back court with the other two players. The advantage of the three-hitter offense is its firepower at the net. With three hitters in the front court, a team has many ways to attack its opponent. The three-hitter attack can be difficult to do, though. New teams should master the two-hitter attack before moving on to the three-hitter attack.

The Importance of a Good Defense

A strong defense is just as important as a strong offense. A strong defense has two main goals. First, the defense receives the opponent's attack. This keeps the opponent from scoring or getting a side-out. Second, a good defense sets up the ball for an attack against the other team. Defensive strategies are designed to achieve both of these goals. The most important part of the defense, though, is to prevent the opponent from scoring or getting control of the ball in a side-out.

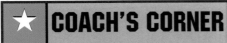

★ COACH'S CORNER

Instead of attacking with a spike every time, try a tip to the corner of your opponents' court to throw them off.

Front court and back court play are important aspects of a good defense. Players in the front court stay one to two feet away from the net, in front of the attack line. The main job of the front court players is to **block** incoming attacks. Back court players stay behind the attack line. Their job is to receive balls that make it past the front court players who are blocking. Base defense is defined as the front court players at the net and the back court players as follows: Right back and left back just behind the 10 foot line and on their respective sides. Middle back deep in the middle of the court.

The back court center moves toward the attack line for a dig.

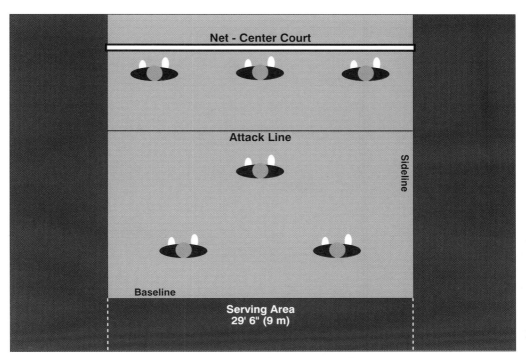

Diagram showing the 2-1-3 defense

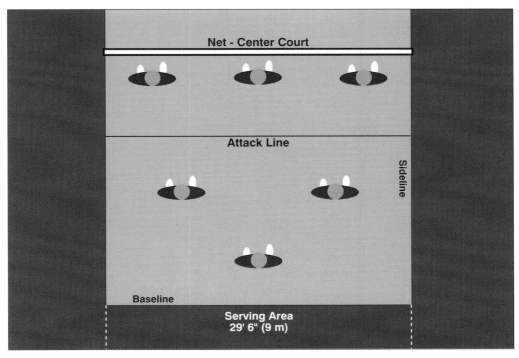

Diagram showing the base defense

Two Defensive Positions

Volleyball uses two defensive positions. One is called 2-1-3 defense. This position places three players in the front court and three in the back court. The front court players stay in a row at the net. Two back court players stay at each side of the court near the end. The third back court player stays in the middle of the court but moves up close to the attack line. This 2-1-3 defense is useful against teams that often use "soft" attacks. The main disadvantage is that it leaves a large part of the court exposed if the ball goes past the front court players.

The second defensive position is usually called 2-4 defense. The 2-4 defense also places three players in the front court and three in the backcourt. The front court players are arranged in a row at the net. The two outside back court players come forward several feet, and the center back court player stays at the end of the court. This position is very effective against teams using hard attacks and spikes. The disadvantage of the 2-4 defense is its difficulty. All players must be ready to receive any type of attack at any moment.

There are many defensive strategies and set-ups. Other more common ones are called perimeter defense and rotation defense. Rotation defense rotates defenders toward the side of the court where the hit takes place.

SERVING AND RECEIVING THE BALL

Serving is one of the most important skills in the game of volleyball. The serve is what actually gets the game going by putting the ball into play. The serve is also the beginning of scoring points. Until the last game of a match, volleyball rules grant points only to the team serving the ball. If the receiving team wins the rally, it gains control of the ball but does not score. During the last game of a match, either side—serving or receiving—can score. This is called rally scoring.

The serve is also important because it is the only part of volleyball that relies completely on individual skill. All other parts of volleyball require team effort to succeed. Remember, points are earned on the serve; and the ball can be lost to the other team during the serve. The individual player who serves must be ready to get the ball over the net every time he or she serves. This is especially important since one player continues serving until his or her team loses the ball. In serving, consistency is the key to success.

Three Basic Serve Techniques

There are many ways to serve the ball. The three most basic are called the **underhand floater**, the **overhand floater**, and the **overhand topspin serve**. The underhand serve is the first type of serve a new player should learn. Advanced players may sometimes use this serve, too. One advantage of the underhand serve is that it is relatively easy to do. Getting the ball over the net and into the opponent's court is not hard to do with the underhand floater. The disadvantage of the underhand serve is its lack of power and speed, making it easy to receive.

★ **DID YOU KNOW?**

When was the last time the U.S. won the Olympic gold medal for volleyball? 1988, Korea. The men's team won.

A player hits an overhand floater.

A player hits an underhand floater.

The overhand floater is more powerful than the underhand serve, making it harder to receive. Serving with the overhand floater causes the ball to move or "float" from side to side or up and down as it travels over the net. This happens because the ball is not stabilized with spin. Receiving the overhand serve is difficult because of this unpredictable motion. The overhand floater is harder to do, however, and must be practiced carefully. The overhand serve is the basis of many advanced serves.

The overhand topspin serve requires more practice. The approach is similar to the topspin floater but upon contact you cause forward spin to the ball, causing it to drop into the opponent's court.

★ COACH'S CORNER

A back row player can attack the ball but only from behind the attack line. Be ready to attack even in the back court.

Receiving the Ball

Receiving the ball is just as important as serving it. The first goal of receiving is defensive. If the serve is not properly received and hits the floor without anyone touching it, the serving team can score a point. This is called an **ace**. Receiving is not just defensive, however. Receiving is the beginning of the offensive attempt to gain control of the ball. Once the receiving team gets the ball, it can begin scoring points. The serve comes quickly and forcefully, so the receiving team must be prepared for action.

Receiving the serve requires several skills. The first is the ability to read a server's moves to predict where the ball will land. Receivers learn to do this by watching the server's feet, hands, and shoulders. Receivers must also learn to recognize which type of serve the server is using. Another skill is calling the serve. If a receiver is prepared to receive the serve, he or she must shout "mine!" or "I've got it!" to alert the others on the team. Only one person can receive the serve; and the team must work together to avoid making an error, or mistake.

A back court player in position to receive an underhand floater.

Setting the ball for a spike.

After a serve is called, the receiver moves into position. The player must move quickly and confidently to be prepared to receive the ball. The player must then set his or her feet, body, shoulders, arms, and hands and pass the ball to the setter. While moving into place and setting, the setter always must keep his or her eyes on the ball. The setter is the player who usually receives the ball from a teammate who passes it. Passing allows a team to prepare for a set and attack against the serving team.

GLOSSARY

ace (AYS) — a serve that scores a point without any opponents touching the ball

attack line (uh TAK LYN) — a line on the court marking 9 feet 10 inches (3 meters) away from the net running from sideline to sideline

attack (uh TAK) — the main offensive move in volleyball

back court (BAK KAWRT) — the area of the court between the attack line and the baseline

block (BLAHK) — the act of stopping a spiked ball, performed by front court players, with hands up and outstretched

center line (SEN ter LYN) — the court marking under the net running from sideline to sideline

front court (FRUNT KAWRT) — area of the court between the net and the attack line

hitter (HIT er) — the player responsible for receiving a set and attacking

lift (LIFT) — a fault in which the ball rests momentarily on a player's hands or forearms

overhand floater (O ver HAND FLO ter) — a more advanced serve, performed with an overhand motion

GLOSSARY

overhand topspin serve (O ver HAND TOP spin SERV) — an advanced serve that causes forward spin to the ball

serve (SERV) — the first hit of the ball over the net to begin a volley

service area (SER vis AIR ee uh) — the entire area behind the baseline from which a serve is made

setter (SET er) — the player responsible for setting the ball to the hitter

sideout (SYD OUT) — a turnover of the ball from the serving to the receiving team in which no points are scored

spike (SPYK) — the attack move, performed by hitting the ball overhand over the net with a downward path

underhand floater (UN der HAND FLO ter) — the basic volleyball serve, performed with an underhand motion

volley (VAHL ee) — the period during which the ball is in play, also a rally

FURTHER READING

Find out more with these helpful books and information sites:

American Coaching Effectiveness Program, Rookie Coaches Volleyball Guide. Champagne, IL: Human Kinetics, 1993.

Fraser, Stephen D. *Strategies for Competitive Volleyball.* New York: Leisure, 1988.

Howard, Robert E. *An Understanding of the Fundamental Techniques of Volleyball.* Needham Heights, MA: Allyn and Bacon, 1996.

Kluka, Darlene, and Dunn, Peter. *Volleyball.* Wm. C. Brown, 1996.

Neville, William S. *Coaching Volleyball Successfully.* New York: Leisure, 1990.

Vierra, Barbara, and Ferguson, Bonnie Jill. *Volleyball: Steps to Success.* Human Kinetics, 1996.

American Volleyball Coaches Association at http://www.volleyball.org/avca/index.html

Complete worldwide source for volleyball information at http://www.volleyball.org/
This site includes descriptions and ordering information for many new books and videos; also, many links.

Great links: http://users.aol.com/vballusa/index.htm

Online Volleyball Magazine subscription page at http://www.volleyballmag.com/sub.htm

More volleyball information at http://www.volleyball.com

INDEX